A WOMAN'S ALMANAC

VOICES FROM NEWFOUNDLAND AND LABRADOR

2017

BREAKWATER
P.O. Box 2188 | St. John's | NL | Canada | A1C 6E6
WWW.BREAKWATERBOOKS.COM

ISBN 978-1-55081-656-3

Every reasonable effort has been made to trace the ownership of material reprinted in this book and to make full acknowledgement for its use. The publisher would be grateful to know of any errors or omissions so they may be rectified in subsequent editions.

We acknowledge the support of the Canada Council for the Arts, which last year invested $153 million to bring the arts to Canadians throughout the country. We acknowledge the financial support of the Government of Canada and the Government of Newfoundland and Labrador through the Department of Business, Tourism, Culture and Rural Development for our publishing activities.
PRINTED AND BOUND IN CANADA.

 Canada Council for the Arts | Conseil des Arts du Canada

Canada

Breakwater Books is committed to choosing papers and materials for our books that help to protect our environment. To this end, this book is printed on a recycled paper that is certified by the Forest Stewardship Council®.

MOON PHASES

 New Moon  First Quarter  Full Moon  Third Quarter

Contents

Introduction

My mother, Florence White, would often say, if you live long enough you will see it all. Well, I sure am happy to live to see the *Almanac* have a second life of its own. I was thrilled when Jenny Wright approached me with the notion that the St. John's Status of Women Council would like to issue the annual *A Woman's Almanac*. I was equally thrilled when she asked me to write this introduction knowing that the *Almanac* is in the capable hands of Breakwater Books. No *Almanac* was ever created without the efforts of a great many women, and I am sure that is the case with this edition.

In 1986 when I began research for the annual agenda book, I hoped this work would inspire other women to tell their stories, or the story of someone remarkable in their lives. It was always such a thrill to see boxes of *Almanacs* arrive, and the subsequent rush to get them distributed to the remote corners of the province and across the country. In 1992, the compendium of all the *Almanac* stories was published in *The Finest Kind*. This continues to be a solid reference tool for our foremothers' stories. For years following this work, I had to resist the urge to interview dynamic women who were accomplishing brilliant things. I kept a thick file of a wish list of women I would have loved to profile. Now I can relax and enjoy the 2017 edition knowing it honours the dynamic, complex and radiant lives of women around us.

My bigger fantasy, while producing this annual book, was that women would find ways to create works of art about other inspiring women; that books would be written based on their lives, films would be made, rugs would be hooked depicting heroic efforts, plays would be written, and all this has happened. In my early years of research, a wonderful web emerged to show how women who achieved their life's dream rarely acted alone. They were part of a network that fuelled them forward. For example, one year I profiled the social activist Julia Salter Earle, another year, Fannie McNeil and later Armine Gosling, women of means at the turn of the twentieth century, who devoted their lives to two things: the betterment of women's place in society and the suffrage cause. Only after the third or fourth year of unearthing their stories did I piece together a puzzle of an era that had virtually been hidden from our history books. Unless I did something to honour that, young women would not know how the right to vote had been won, or of the courageous women who ran to be members of the municipal council or the legislature. Thus the docu-drama, *The Untold Story of the Suffragists of Newfoundland*, was born. It took five years to create this film, but that was minor given it was a thirty-year struggle for women to gain the right to vote in 1925. Since this film was released in 2000, several women have become members of the House of Assembly, including my good friend, Gerry Rogers, who was profiled in the 1992 *Almanac*. Ninety years after the vote was won, Trudy Morgan-Cole published the novel *A Sudden Sun*. She weaves a compelling tapestry based on the lives and emotional struggles of young suffragists between the 1890s and 1925. I greatly admire writers who can dive into an era and create fiction from the fact of their lives.

For every edition of the *Almanac*, several banker boxes of research was compiled. Thanks to the MUN Provincial Archives, you can now open one of those boxes virtually and look at the detail and astonishing work these women accomplished. Thanks to their hard work, today there are women police officers, engineers, women playing hockey on a highly competitive level, women doctors, lawyers and leaders in all aspects of our society. This is vital if we are to evolve to the level of living we deserve. This includes a balance of the wealth that is all too often afforded to one level of society.

We want a wild and wonderful world for our young women, but we also want to carve out a place to live independent and creative lives to our last breath. By celebrating ourselves we empower each other. We are not waiting for an epitaph of a few words to summarize a life well lived, we are celebrating now, caring for each other and knowing that by caring we will attain a quality of life all those women before us worked toward.

As a grandmother of three dynamic children, passing on strength through our stories, acknowledging and celebrating our achievements is even more important. This *Almanac* is a record in our own words, of our own lives—how good is that?

With this edition I can relax and enjoy the read and the year ahead. I hope you do too. Congratulations SJSWC.

Marian Frances White

RUTH LAWRENCE

Ruth Lawrence's work as an actor, writer, and filmmaker has taken her to Ireland, France, the US, and across Canada. As an actor, she has performed over 100 roles, mostly in their premiere production with companies such as Rising Tide, Home-First, Tarragon, RCAT, Wreckhouse, White Rooster, Wonderbolt, C2C, She Said Yes, NAX, NYPT, Treetop, and Showboat Theatre. She has directed eight professional productions including ***West Moon***, ***Fragrance of Sorrow*** and the ***Joan Morrissey Story*** (RTT), ***Possible Maps*** (RCAT), ***Proud*** (Double Sure). She is Artistic Director of White Rooster Theatre (www.whiteroostertheatre.com). She is a past recipient of The Rhonda Payne Theatre Award, and ***It Is Solved by Walking***, a WRT show she co-produced in 2014, received five Merritt Award nominations in NS.

Her award-winning short ***Talus & Scree*** was a national semi-finalist in CBCs Short Film Face Off, reached #1 in the Short of the Month for February 2015 (with a Best Editor nomination), and was an official selection for the 2014 WIFT International Showcase. Her short films have screened across Canada and the US. Since 2014, she has produced three short films for Blue Pinion Films: RBC MJ Award winning shorts ***Before the War*** and ***The Tour***; and ***Quelle Affaire*** (an iPhone short she also wrote and directed), and is a co-producer with Pope Productions on the feature ***Hunting Pignut***. She is the co-creator and director of the five-episode webseries ***Buy the Boards***, released March 2014 (www.buy-the-boards.com). Ruth won the 2011 Joan Orenstein Best Actress Award for ***Clipper Gold*** at the Atlantic Film Festival and the 2011 RBC Michelle Jackson Award for Emerging Filmmaker for ***Two Square Feet***, starring Jeanne Beker. She was named the Newfoundland and Labrador Arts Council's 2011 Artist of the Year, in 2013 was honoured with the Queen's Jubilee Medal, and recently received the 2016 YWCA Woman of Distinction Award for Arts & Culture.

ON Joan Morrissey

PHOTO COURTESY OF THE MORRISSEY FAMILY

"She was the easiest person to work with…she was conscientious about her work. She was always anxious to help local performers who were just coming up…promoting Newfoundlanders was one of her main interests." These were some of the words producer Dave Lawrence used to describe her in a *Newfoundland Herald* tribute published just days after her death in 1978. Spoken in the wake of her devastating loss, it captures only one facet of the gem Joan Morrissey. At the age of forty-three, Joan had accomplished more than many would even attempt in her day. Working in theatre, TV, radio, and playing regular musical gigs as a devoted mother to a family of six children is almost unimaginable today. Yet imagine she did, and work was no stranger to this enigmatic performer who made her singing debut at the age of nine.

Those familiar with the *Woman's Almanac* will know that she has been here before, first featured in 1989 through the words of her daughter, who would go on to write a book on her well-loved mother. Through that piece, we were brought inside the Morrissey home and much was revealed about the richness of their family life. When I was asked to consider a woman who influenced me for the revival of the *Almanac* (which had a daily presence in my bag for years), Joan was chosen because her impact, so many years later, continues to ripple out to those of us who dream of artistic expression that actually puts food on the table. It should be unthinkable, but for women especially, the struggles have not changed that much, no matter what part of the creative world we work in.

First introduced to her over the radio waves, as girls in rural Newfoundland, my friends and I all knew the words to "The Mobile

Goat" and "The Boarding House on Federation Square." The songs Joan sang spoke to our experience, our love of stories, and our humour. It would be years later before I learned of the circumstances of her death. Reconciling this remarkable woman who spent much of her time bringing light to others with the one who took her life in a period of extreme darkness was difficult. Once we live and hold close others as they struggle, we can come to realize that there are many questions we may never answer, some decisions we may not ever understand. We continue to love, just the same. I love everything Joan Morrissey brought into my life. Many, many others would offer a comparable testimonial. Still, none of us can know the true depth of the woman.

Joan was performing and recording before I was born, and yet she remains an incredible influence, a pioneer who trod down a path for performers who would come after her. Besides owning her records and watching her shows, many Newfoundlanders would remember her from her days hosting the morning talk show *Newfoundland This A.M.* and the mid-afternoon *Today* shows on CJON-TV from 1973-74. Her natural charm and ability to get along well with all kinds of people made her a first-class interviewer. Around this time, she also hosted the channel's prime-time *Talent Showcase* series.

The life of this extraordinary woman has been well documented. For three nights in November 1993, fortunate audiences were delighted to see and hear Vicky Hynes's portrayal in *Joan Morrissey Remembered* by Rick Moriarity. I recall sitting in the auditorium and being transported, theatrically, by the songs and spirit embodied in the work she created in her lifetime. A very personal and beautiful account of her professional and family life was revealed in the touching book *Yes My Dear* by her daughter, Debbie Morrissey Stafford, in 2003. Not long after, multi-talented writer/performers Susan Kent and Jody Richardson wrote and premiered the autobiographical play *So Lets Bring on Our Favourite*, and it was produced at Rising Tide Theatre in Trinity to much acclaim.

Working in that theatre, I became enthralled by her life story. I was honoured to direct a remount of the production with the superb talent Petrina Bromley and a wonderful supporting cast. Spending that much time with Joan's legacy inspired a different kind of respect. Not the distant admiration of a fan who knows only the recorded song or well-rehearsed production, but not only the daily grind of the artist and her collaborator's daily labour either. I discovered the respect that can come from an examination of a life lived that doesn't resolve the enigma of that complex artist but subsequently reels us in tighter to its lovable and intriguing subject. Like the recurring rehearsals for a play, Joan's legacy deserves repeated exploration. She knew that being successful here often means leading a full life wearing many hats. She folded laundry and earned a Juno nomination. She led a brownie pack and rehearsed a musical with a broken leg. She helped with homework and mentored emerging artists. She was woven into the fabric of our culture through radio broadcasts of her voice and music. Joan Morrissey is remembered as a woman, mother, wife, and best friend whose enormous body of work rooted her firmly as Newfoundland's First Lady of Song.

JANUARY

1 SUNDAY

New Year's Day

2 MONDAY

New Year's Day Statutory Holiday

3 TUESDAY

4 WEDNESDAY

5 THURSDAY

6 FRIDAY

Epiphany (Old Christmas Day)

7 SATURDAY

NOTES

JANUARY

8 SUNDAY

9 MONDAY

10 TUESDAY

11 WEDNESDAY

12 THURSDAY

13 FRIDAY

14 SATURDAY

CASSIE EILEEN BROWN: Born in Rose Blanche on **January 10, 1919**, journalist, editor, and author of *Death on the Ice* (1972).

JANUARY

15 SUNDAY

16 MONDAY

17 TUESDAY

18 WEDNESDAY

JANUARY

19 THURSDAY

20 FRIDAY

21 SATURDAY

NOTES

JANUARY

22 SUNDAY

23 MONDAY

24 TUESDAY

25 WEDNESDAY

26 THURSDAY

27 FRIDAY 

28 SATURDAY

Chinese New Year

SHIRLEY GOUNDRY, who was a founding member of the Newfoundland Status of Women Council, passes away in **January 2006**.

JANUARY FEBRUARY

29 SUNDAY

30 MONDAY

31 TUESDAY

1 WEDNESDAY

FEBRUARY

2 THURSDAY

Groundhog Day

3 FRIDAY

4 SATURDAY

NOTES

ELIZABETH PENASHUE

PHOTO BY CAMILLE FOUILLARD

Elizabeth Penashue is a seventy-one year old Innu environmental activist. She had been in jail more times than she can remember. She has received an Honourary Doctorate from Memorial University of Newfoundland and a National Aboriginal Achievement Award for her work preserving the language and culture of the Innu people. Mrs. Penashue has two daughters and seven sons, fifty-three grandchildren and twenty-three great-grandchildren. A collection of extracts from her journals will be published in 2016. She will continue to lead travels by foot and canoe through the Labrador interior as long as she is able.

A Labrador Innu woman who inspired me and still does:

This is the story of my late sister, Rose Gregoire, who passed away March 14, 2007, at the very young age of fifty-eight years old.

My sister worked for many years as a community-service worker for the Department of Social Services, as it was called back then. She was a very well-respected community member. She spent her days helping her people, especially women and children in abusive situations. Although we all knew that our sister was sometimes tired, her door was always open to help anybody who needed help. Rose took great pride in helping people, not just the Innu, but all people. If you ask those who knew her or worked with her, they will all tell you what a wonderful person she was.

When we were younger, we travelled to Nutshimit with our parents. She was much younger but I remember she too very much enjoyed being there. Out in the country we were taught how to clean animals, and how to take care of ourselves in the tent. We would always go with our mom, picking boughs, fishing, and snaring rabbits. It was a time to learn; she took what she could remember and taught her children.

ON Rose Gregoire

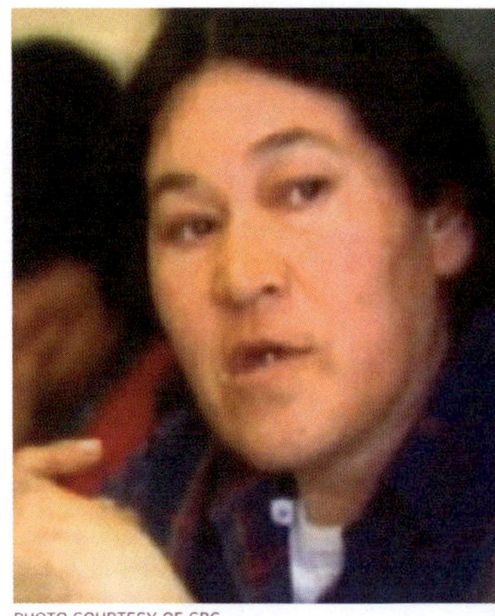
PHOTO COURTESY OF CBC

When we were in Nutshimit, we never ran out of things to do or play, we always had something to do.

Even though my sister did not spend as much time in Nutshimit as I did, I had much respect for her. She was knowledgeable about the world in ways I wasn't. She spoke English and learned how to read and write in that language, and before she went to work with Social Services, she trained in St John's to be a Licenced Practical Nurse.

When the struggle against NATO began for the Innu people in the early 80s, she was one of the women who spent time in jail, fighting for the land and the future of all Innu children. Rose had four children of her own, two girls and two boys, and she loved them dearly. When she was blessed with grandchildren, she was overjoyed with happiness. She loved them all very much.

She did her best to teach her children and grandchildren about her belief in the Innu culture and to have respect for the language. I remember her teaching her oldest granddaughter, Nykesha, to make Innu bread. She was only a little girl, maybe seven years old, and Rose was so proud when she learned. She praised her, and her granddaughter was delighted with the praise. Nykesha asked her grandmother, "Will we make more bread?" and my sister Rose said yes. It is a memory that is very special for me. She was a wonderful grandmother to her grandchildren.

Over the years she travelled with me and other women from our community to talk about our culture and our struggles as a people. She translated for me on many occasions and she also would help me write to people in English.

When my sister Rose was tired, and needed a break, she would ask me and our sister, Ann Philomena, to go to our tents, which were just off the highway. She would say, "Let's go to the tent and talk about the past, and have a good laugh." We would take her with us and we always had a good time together. She always did her best to maintain her home, cooking and cleaning. Sometimes she would invite women to her home to have a meal; I guess it was her way of giving them a break.

Rose was always there for me. I always knew I could count on her to help me. If I was sad, and I needed to talk, she would listen. If I had a dream she would help me to interpret my dream.

One year, when I was on one of my walks, the people who accompanied me decided that they wanted to go back to the community before we finished. I was very upset and sad so I asked my husband to deliver a letter to Rose telling her about the group that wanted to leave. As soon as she got that letter, she went over to our other sister's house and asked Ann Philomena to continue the walk with me. My sister Ann Philomena respected Rose very much, also. I continued my walk that year and finished it because of Rose and Ann Philomena.

Rose always pushed me to be a better person; there are many things in my life I could have not done without her encouragement and love. Thank you, Rose, for your friendship and your sisterhood.

NOTES

PHOTO COURTESY OF ST. JOHN'S STATUS OF WOMEN COUNCIL ARCHIVES

FEBRUARY

5 SUNDAY

6 MONDAY

7 TUESDAY

8 WEDNESDAY

FEBRUARY

9 THURSDAY

10 FRIDAY

11 SATURDAY

NOTES

FEBRUARY

12 SUNDAY

13 MONDAY

14 TUESDAY

Valentine's Day

15 WEDNESDAY

FEBRUARY

16 THURSDAY

17 FRIDAY

18 SATURDAY

NOTES

FEBRUARY

19 SUNDAY

20 MONDAY

21 TUESDAY

22 WEDNESDAY

FEBRUARY

23 THURSDAY

24 FRIDAY

25 SATURDAY

In response to the funding cuts that impacted all NL Women's Centres, the **SJSWC** holds an emergency community meeting on **February 22, 1990**, to rally supporters.

FEBRUARY MARCH

26 SUNDAY 

27 MONDAY

28 TUESDAY

Shrove Tuesday (Pancake Day)

1 WEDNESDAY

Ash Wednesday

MARCH

2 THURSDAY

3 FRIDAY

4 SATURDAY

After ten years of research, advocacy, committee and volunteer work, on **February 29, 2012**, **MARGUERITE'S PLACE** has its grand opening.

AMELIA CURRAN

PHOTO BY HEATHER POLLOCK

They Promised You Mercy is the newest collection of songs by Amelia Curran, Canada's master contemporary songstress. On this album, Amelia's knife-sharp lyrics find peace and even cheerfulness amidst lush layers provided by producer Michael Phillip Wojewoda's nuanced studio vision. The album is a poised, focused and consummate work that showcases Amelia's singular songwriting talent. ***They Promised You Mercy*** raises the lyrical bar yet again with its unrivaled eloquence. ***They Promised You Mercy*** was nominated for the 2015 Juno Award for Roots and Traditional Album of the Year.

Amelia Curran received her first Juno Award for ***Hunter, Hunter*** in front of an adoring hometown crowd in St. John's, NL, in April 2010. The album, which solidified Amelia's reputation as an heir to Leonard Cohen's songwriting throne, also received a total of four ECMA nominations, four Music NL awards, three Music NS awards, a spot on ***Exclaim***'s Wood, Wires & Whiskey coveted year-end and a place on the 2010 Polaris Long List. With the release of ***Spectators*** in 2012, Amelia was once again nominated for a Juno Award for Roots and Traditional Album of the Year. The album is a meditation on frailty, restlessness, time and its finitudes, and is both storm and harbour to Amelia's celebrated lyricism. The record received rave reviews and found its way on to many Best of 2012 lists across Canada.

Some people are tidal pools. They attract, nurture, protect. And everything within luminous and rife with community and loveliness.

Edythe would point at me from across the room and keep her finger poised as she crossed the crowd. Then, close enough to be heard, demanded to know when I'd be coming to her Winterset Writers Festival. It was more an accusation than an invitation. And for some time I protested, claiming not to be a writer, which would earn me a good telling to, and leave me bashful and full of responsibility.

ON Edythe Goodridge

PHOTO BY RONALD AYLES

She didn't accept self-doubt from me and she didn't accept it from any artist. She tracked down those things that threaten to keep us quiet or unable to live, challenged and changed those forces. Censorship, assessment, funding, and a very clear sense of worth.

Now, if you didn't know, here is the tip of the iceberg: A cultural administrator, journalist, program developer with MUN Extension, curator of the MUN Art Gallery (which became the Art Gallery of Newfoundland and Labrador), founder of the Winterset Festival and Literary Award, FIRST executive director of the Newfoundland and Labrador Arts Council, Director of Visual Arts at the Canada Council, and that's just the titles.

Unofficially, Edythe Goodridge is known as the Mother of Newfoundland and Labrador. She attracted artists, nurtured us, protected us. Tied us to a totem and waved us around like sparklers.

Those in the Newfoundland Renaissance in the 1970s would have witnessed her championship of us first hand. When members of Lukey's Boat shipped off to England and the rag tag group of friends that followed returned home some time later and Figgy Duff, The Wonderful Grand Band, and CODCO would follow. No small drop of culture there. Mind you, her championship was as Newfoundland in its nature as her character—not challenging or aggressive, but loving, matter-of-fact and with a sense of humour. When Edythe first heard a young Ron Hynes, for instance, she described him as "some young fellow down Ferryland way…a bit rough around the edges…" And no small drop of culture there either.

There's no telling if they had any idea how important all that would be to us now. And without Edythe, much of our homegrown artists and their work would have fallen away and we'd have grown up on imported art and culture from Canada, Britain, and America, and celebrated artists like Gerald Squires would be little known eccentrics about Town.

Now, there are no lack of times we have to defend ourselves as artists. We have to gather and fight to stay afloat in a sea of budget cuts and economic strife. We repeat ourselves every few years, reminding the city, the province, and the country, the value of art and culture.

What sets Edythe apart from all that fuss is there's none of her work was ever in anger or defence. The vision was plain. We are Newfoundland and Labrador. Come gather round and see. Art is not simply an entertainment, not a novelty of a night out or a crafty keepsake for your come-from-aways. Art is here to provide you, to build you up and tear you down, to bring us together and define us, to help us grow and shift, to remember and remain. It is the singular most important thing to who we are.

If I had the opportunity now to say Thank You, it wouldn't near be enough, and still she would just laugh at me, grab me by the back of the neck and direct me, steer me like a wheelbarrow, to someone she thought I should meet.

I'd known Edythe most of my life. She and my father, David Curran, were colleagues at MUN Extension. But it wasn't until I finally had the nerve to perform at the Winterset Festival in 2007 that I began to understand how much I loved being loved by Edythe. Because quite simply, my father was impressed and delighted that I had been included by her. It said to him that I was going to be alright, because the Mother of Newfoundland believed in me.

She'd tell me to knock it off. She'd ask when am I going to visit the girls in Salvage for a game of cards and a few too many drinks. And not-so-quietly drop a new idea, a new project into the midst of us. And all the time laughing and carrying on, proving to us our limitlessness and beauty.

NOTES

PHOTO COURTESY OF ST. JOHN'S STATUS OF WOMEN COUNCIL ARCHIVES

MARCH

5 SUNDAY 

6 MONDAY

7 TUESDAY

8 WEDNESDAY

International Women's Day

MARCH

9 THURSDAY

10 FRIDAY

11 SATURDAY

DORA OAKE RUSSELL: Born in Change Islands on **March 7, 1912**. Dora was the first woman editor of ***The Evening Telegram***, and profiled many local women in her regular column "Woman of the Week."

MARCH

12 SUNDAY ○

Daylight Saving Time Begins

13 MONDAY

Commonwealth Day

14 TUESDAY

15 WEDNESDAY

16 THURSDAY

17 FRIDAY

St. Patrick's Day

18 SATURDAY

NOTES

MARCH

19 SUNDAY

20 MONDAY 

Equinox

21 TUESDAY

22 WEDNESDAY

MARCH

23 THURSDAY

24 FRIDAY

25 SATURDAY

NOTES

MARCH

26 SUNDAY

27 MONDAY 

28 TUESDAY

29 WEDNESDAY

MARCH APRIL

30 THURSDAY

31 FRIDAY

1 SATURDAY

NOTES

GERRY ROGERS

PHOTO BY NED PRATT

Gerry is an unabashedly proud feminist activist and documentary filmmaker with over twenty films and more than forty international awards to her credit, among them two Geminis. In October 2011 Gerry was the first "out" lesbian elected to the NL House of Assembly. MHA for St. John's Centre, she is part of the "small but mighty" NDP Caucus. She focuses on issues affecting women, seniors, LGBTQ2S community, mental health and addictions, housing and anti-poverty issues. Gerry was born in Corner Brook in 1956 and lives in St. John's with her equally proud feminist activist partner of twenty-five years, Peg Norman.

It's fall of 1980. I'm in my last year of a Social Work degree at MUN. Iris Kirby at the Women's Program, Secretary of State Canada is my field placement supervisor. I'm twenty-four, have never been a part of the "women's movement," but already seeing that the world is pretty different for women and girls than it is for men and boys. I had one prof who talked about housing and poverty and how it related specifically to women. I was starting to get the picture.

Iris takes me to the Women's Centre of the Newfoundland Status of Women Council* on Military Road, an old modest three-storey typical St. John's row house. They're having a province-wide women's conference and I'm supposed to help organize it. I'm terrified... a lot terrified. I'd heard they were all bra-burning, man-hating angry women who don't use make up. I kind of knew it wasn't true...but hey it was 1980! Iris knew all this was going to be new to me. She counselled me to listen and observe and after the meeting we would debrief.

* *The name was changed to St. John's Status of Women Council in 1984.*

ON Iris Kirby

PHOTO COURTESY OF IRIS KIRBY HOUSE FOUNDATION

Crowded into the front room were a few board members—Billie Thurston, Bonnie James, Wendy Williams, Jill Schooley, Judy Tuddiver, Cathy Coffin, Marion Atkinson, and Barbara Doran, the only staff member. There was a lot of work to do. The date and location had been set, Hotel Newfoundland. Nova Scotia singer/songwriter Rita MacNeil was booked and coming, but the workshop topics and schedule had to be finalized and billets needed to be found for the dozens of women coming from across the province. Most of the discussion centered around how some of the workshop topics would be described, who would lead them, and whether the media would be allowed in. There were sessions on childcare, equal pay for equal work, the inequities of the Matrimonial Property Act and do-it-yourself divorce, there was child poverty, violence against women and then the more contentious issues of abortion and sexual orientation. It was after all 1980!

These women knew their stuff. They laughed, they argued, they proposed, made decisions, argued again, changed decisions and laughed again. They were on the cutting edge of the women's movement in Newfoundland and they knew it. They were firebrands and they were part of setting the agenda for the revolution! I was in awe. And my life changed!

What a privilege it was to be allowed in, even though so much was new to me, allowed in to be part of this women's movement occupied by courageous feminists who were determined to change the world, to make it better for all women against all odds. They taught me and mentored me. I listened and absorbed. I heard the stories of women who were badly treated by discriminatory divorce laws, women who had been sexually assaulted and had nowhere to go, women trying to work outside the house but couldn't afford childcare, women who had been cut off from Social Assistance because they had a boyfriend, women who were being beaten at home and had nowhere to go.

And these fearless feminists worked, worked so hard together. They taught each other, they read Mary Daly, Phyllis Chester, Robin Morgan's *Sisterhood is Powerful* and they lived it. They wrote the first "Do It Yourself Divorce Kit," they were the first women's centre in Canada to buy their own building, they started the first Transition House for "battered women" on Garrison Hill, they pushed for pay equity, helped start the first abortion clinic in the province with Dr. Henry Morgentaler, started the Rape Crisis Centre, and they lobbied to get the Matrimonial Property Act changed to be more equitable for women.

In 1981, I graduated and was offered a job as co-coordinator of the Women's Centre with Barbara Doran. Together with the board and members of the Newfoundland Status of Women Council we continued to take on the world. We had CR groups (consciousness raising groups), TGIFs. We laughed, cried, argued, mentored each other. We were on fire! And it was exciting! Change was happening!

The amazing feminist activists of the St. John's Status of Women Council were changing the world! And they changed my life. Courageous, passionate and compassionate women! Thank you Iris Kirby, Billie Thurston, Bonnie James, Wendy Williams, Jill Schooley, Judy Tuddiver, Cathy Coffin, Marion Atkinson, Lilianne Bouzane, Fran Innes and Barbara Doran. Firebrands, sisters, resisters…

And then there was Clause 28, a notwithstanding clause that would protect our rights and freedoms in our Canadian Charter of Rights and Freedoms. Women across the country had fought hard for and won it…But that's another story….

NOTES

PHOTO COURTESY OF ST. JOHN'S STATUS OF WOMEN COUNCIL ARCHIVES

APRIL

2 SUNDAY

3 MONDAY

4 TUESDAY

5 WEDNESDAY

APRIL

6 THURSDAY

7 FRIDAY

8 SATURDAY

NOTES

APRIL

9 SUNDAY

Vimy Ridge Day

10 MONDAY

11 TUESDAY ○

First Day of Passover

12 WEDNESDAY

APRIL

13 THURSDAY

Maundy Thursday

14 FRIDAY

Good Friday

15 SATURDAY

Women gain the right to vote and hold public office in Newfoundland and Labrador on **April 13, 1925**, though this right was only extended to white women at the time.

APRIL

16 SUNDAY

Easter Sunday

17 MONDAY

Easter Monday

18 TUESDAY

Last Day of Passover

19 WEDNESDAY

APRIL

20 THURSDAY

21 FRIDAY

22 SATURDAY

NOTES

APRIL

23 SUNDAY

24 MONDAY

St. George's Day

25 TUESDAY

26 WEDNESDAY 

APRIL

27 THURSDAY

28 FRIDAY

29 SATURDAY

NOTES

APRIL MAY

30 SUNDAY

1 MONDAY

2 TUESDAY

3 WEDNESDAY

MAY

4 THURSDAY

5 FRIDAY

6 SATURDAY

NOTES

KABERI SARMA-DEBNATH

Kaberi Sarma-Debnath, a registered Social Worker and Researcher, is the Executive Director of the Multicultural Women's Organization of Newfoundland and Labrador (MWONL)—a non-profit organization based in St. John's, NL. In this role, she leads the innovative culturally appropriate gender-based programs to assist and empower newcomers, immigrant women and families in the province in its second decade of service. She started her career as a Social Work professor in a university college and later joined Health and Community Services–St. John's region. In her community, she works with the issues, including violence against women and older immigrants: employment challenges, settlement and integration, seniors issues and human rights. She is the editor of MWONL Newsletter ***Sharing Thoughts***. Being the training manager of MWONL's Trans-cultural Competency and Awareness Training (TCCA), she has been invited to the university and various organizations as a guest speaker, providing cultural competency training to educators and health-care professionals and other service providers all the year round. She's published two books, produced more than ten reports and several articles for newspapers and other magazines.

ON Yamuna Kutty

PHOTO COURTESY OF YAMUNA KUTTY

My close friend for over a decade, Yamuna Kutty, is a woman who is a highly inspirational force in my life. Yamuna was born in India and moved to Newfoundland in 1968. She raised two children along with her beloved husband, Madhavan, who passed away in 2011. She is the current Vice-President of the Multicultural Women's Organization of Newfoundland and Labrador and a Council Member on the Provincial Advisory Council on the Status of Women.

After retiring from her job as an administrator at Memorial University's Department of Community Medicine, rather than taking it easy, Yamuna chose to dedicate her time to various committees and community development work. Over the years, she was on the boards of the St. John's Status of Women Council, the National Action Committee on the Status of Women, and the National Organization of Immigrant and Visible Minority Women of Canada, among others. Her major areas of focus are critical perspectives about the lives of immigrant and refugee women and conquering violence against women and children.

Yamuna always says, "Be passionate and honestly enjoy what you do in life! If you don't, you need to try something else. Also don't be afraid to ask for help. It's amazing, but you'll actually get it." These are particularly inspiring phrases for me. Not so long ago, I thought asking for help was a sign of weakness. Now I've learned that asking for help is a strength; it builds your personal information network, teaches you trust and aids you in resolving issues.

Yamuna credits her parents and in-laws with making her the authentic and genuine person she is and has extreme gratitude to them. She notes that they were simple decent people who valued honesty and integrity. She always says, "Be truthful to yourself and others that you deal with. One set of lies calls for more sets of lies until you are lost in the maze, giving you a cause to hang your head in shame. Let your conscience be your guide."

The most critical lesson she has taught me is to believe in myself. If you believe in yourself, you will shine and glow! I feel that this has made me into a more efficient and empathetic service provider. I learned to stand up and accept challenges and take control of life. I now strive to empower those newcomer women who lack confidence and believe themselves inferior. Yamuna says, "Hold your head high and have confidence; you are just as beautiful and worthy as the next person." As I write this piece, I am reminded that I have walked a number of paths on life's journey thus far. Although I have conquered some challenges, there are still cliffs to scale and mountains to climb. From Yamuna I have learned to climb the ladder of success, believing in myself, with one arm reaching upwards and the other always lending a hand to those just below. This propagates the cycle; it grows you and future generations.

Yamuna is an authentic friend. She listens to other people's views in a positive and respectful manner. She compliments and encourages me but is not afraid to provide constructive feedback to assist me with challenging projects, helping me to achieve high standards. She is always there for me—in my good days and bad days. She is a true leader and guides people who need direction. She is kind, sincere and honest.

I would like to extend my gratitude to this great woman for her friendship and inspiration. She has expanded my horizons, energized my personal and professional life, and most importantly, this wonderful lady has helped me to discover my inner spirit!

NOTES

PHOTO COURTESY OF ST. JOHN'S STATUS OF WOMEN COUNCIL ARCHIVES

MAY

7 SUNDAY

8 MONDAY

9 TUESDAY

10 WEDNESDAY ○

11 THURSDAY

12 FRIDAY

13 SATURDAY

HELENA SQUIRES becomes the first woman elected to the Newfoundland House of Assembly on **May 17, 1930**.

MAY

14 SUNDAY

Mother's Day

15 MONDAY

16 TUESDAY

17 WEDNESDAY

18 THURSDAY 

19 FRIDAY

20 SATURDAY

MARGARET ALEXANDRA SHEA: The first professionally trained nurse in Newfoundland and Labrador. Shea was also the first woman recorded to own a car in Newfoundland. She died on **May 18, 1949**.

MAY

21 SUNDAY

22 MONDAY

Victoria Day

23 TUESDAY

24 WEDNESDAY

MAY

25 THURSDAY 

26 FRIDAY

27 SATURDAY

Ramadan Begins

LADY CONSTANCE MARIA HARRIS: Lady Harris directed the Women's Patriotic Association, and through the WPA launched the Outport Nursing Scheme on **May 20, 1920**. The ONS recruited and employed five professional midwives from England to serve outport communities of Newfoundland and Labrador.

MAY

28 SUNDAY

29 MONDAY

30 TUESDAY

31 WEDNESDAY

JUNE

1 THURSDAY 

2 FRIDAY

3 SATURDAY

NOTES

FLORENCE BUTTON

My love of history is large in my life landscape. Much of my writing reaches into the past, both poetry and prose. My research has resulted in two historical plays, one of which has an excerpt in the Grade Eight Newfoundland and Labrador Studies Textbook. ***Connecting Rooms*** tells of the life and times of the women of the Labrador fishery. I'm presently working on an historical children's book and an adult novel. One of my poems will be read this summer at the Cenotaph in Carbonear on July 1, to commemorate the Battle of Beaumont Hamel.

In my seasonal day job, I manage and provide interpretation for two Museum Exhibits, direct the Carbonear Historic Walking Tours (Winner of a provincial Manning Award) and work with students who also act in our walking tours and interpret during the summer at our museums. I volunteer with the Carbonear Library Board of Directors, St. Patrick's Organic Community Garden, and enjoy being a contributing poet at our "Let's Talk Poetry Group."

I am a woman at a place in life who counts and names with gratitude her greatest blessings: family, faith, friends, health, contentment and opportunities to always learn. Lifelong learning is very important to me, and research and writing allow entry and exploration into worlds of infinite possibility. I seek to know more of the experiences of those who came before us and continue to search for opportunities to look, listen and learn from their wisdom.

It cannot get better than that.

ON Women of the Labrador Fishery

I was born in a small community in Trinity Bay: Sibley's Cove. My parents were Gordon and Florence (Squires) Button, both of whom were involved in the inshore fishery. The fabric of all my memories is interwoven with the work of my mother, Flossie, and most of the other women of Sibley's Cove, who all either headed, gutted, salted, spread or picked up the fish from June until October, all the while, raising families, making and baking batches of bread, washing laundry for a houseful,weeding gardens, turning over the hay, cooking meals and nursing babies. At the time it was part of the landscape of life and none of it warranted special notice.

I read historical material, research, write and provide historical interpretation sometimes. While researching for an exhibit about Carbonear's connection to the Labrador fishery, more than a decade ago, I interviewed some fishermen who had been participants in the Labrador fishery. During some of these interviews, the wives were present, and occasionally interjected tidbits about their experiences in the Labrador fishery. Long after the exhibit work was completed, I could not forget the stories, and perhaps because I grew up in what were actually the end times of an era (unbeknown to us innocents, then) I was filled with a deep admiration for these women of the Labrador fishery and indeed as I am with all women who have worked in this industry.

When an opportunity arose to write a play concerning women's work, it seemed that I must write a play which detailed the lives of women and their work in an industry that demanded mighty women. I knew exactly who some of the mightiest of these women were and had also learned of some others who blazed the trail.

As I wrote, it was almost as though the women were standing beside me, and indeed I have no doubt that some of them were. As I slowly developed each character, I read it aloud and became each voice, and consequently, as I wrote, the voices told the story. And in *Connecting Rooms—A Tribute*, it is their voices you hear, spoken in the Newfoundland vernacular, as they would.

How these women have inspired me! I admire their devotion, integrity, determination and the indomitable spirit that flamed in each one. I am awed by an inherent work ethic that neither asked for, nor expected anything, thinking only of their children, their families, and that they be fed, warmed and clothed. Indeed they were selfless and in many ways, especially in the first half of the nineteenth century, faceless.

In my personal research, I read of one, Mrs. Susannah Grant Bemister, who began travelling to the Labrador fishery with her husband and children as early as the 1820s. She raised a family of nine children while yearly participating in the rigours of the Labrador fishery until her death in 1859. Mrs. Bemister, in preparation (and doubtless many others), would begin to gather and pack all that was needed by late May, because the journey to the Labrador fishery would begin in very early June. Susannah must have been incredibly organized because knowing that she would not return to her home until at least mid-October, it clearly was a monumental task. Consider the necessities required for nearly five months for a family of eleven: food, bedding, clothing, pots and pans and many other utilitarian items needed for daily living. Sometimes the goat and a few chickens would be caged on the deck of the schooners so that the children had milk and eggs when and where there was none. These women would work alongside the men, at the fishery, and cared for all hands with no medical or spiritual guidance available from June until October. Then everything must be packed again for the return journey by sea, from the coast of the Labrador, and October was well known for stormy weather. It was not unusual for ships with whole families to be lost in these autumn gales. I mention Susannah because she represents many early women, who were true pioneers in our own provincial history.

The women of the fishing industry of Newfoundland and Labrador, past and present, have inspired me in many ways. I am honoured to give them a voice in *Connecting Rooms – A Tribute*, and I chose the month of June because that would have been the month when they physically began the summer's work, both in the inshore and Labrador fishery. I'm proud that I have known some personally, and having learned of the others I will always be very grateful and proud to say that and to give them a voice.

PHOTO COURTESY OF ST. JOHN'S STATUS OF WOMEN COUNCIL ARCHIVES

JUNE

4 SUNDAY

5 MONDAY

6 TUESDAY

7 WEDNESDAY

8 THURSDAY

9 FRIDAY ○

10 SATURDAY

SHANAWDITHIT, thought to be the last of the Beothuks, dies in St. John's on **June 6, 1829**.

JUNE

11 SUNDAY

12 MONDAY

13 TUESDAY

14 WEDNESDAY

15 THURSDAY

16 FRIDAY

17 SATURDAY

NOTES

JUNE

18 SUNDAY

Father's Day

19 MONDAY

20 TUESDAY

21 WEDNESDAY

Summer Solstice | National Aboriginal Day

JUNE

22 THURSDAY

23 FRIDAY 

24 SATURDAY

Midsummer's Day

NOTES

JUNE

25 SUNDAY

26 MONDAY

Discovery Day

27 TUESDAY

28 WEDNESDAY

JUNE JULY

29 THURSDAY

30 FRIDAY 

1 SATURDAY

Canada Day | Memorial Day

ST. JOHN'S STATUS OF WOMEN COUNCIL (Then Newfoundland Status of Women Council) opened the Women's Centre on 83 Military Road on **June 25, 1978**. This was the first Women's Centre in Canada to be owned by its members, and the longest continuously running Centre in the country.

SUSAN SHINER

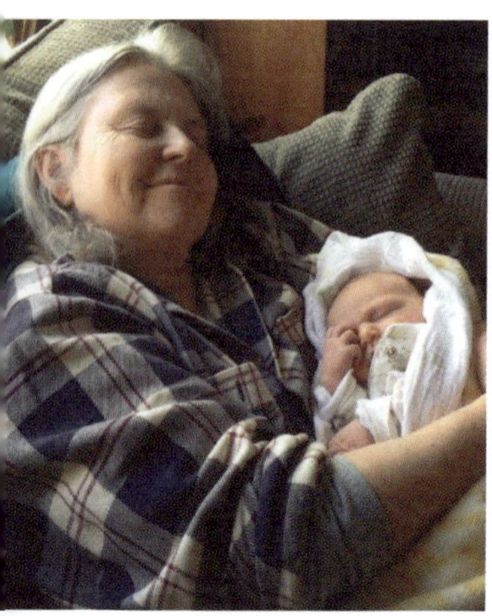
PHOTO COURTESY OF SUSAN SHINER

I have been involved with SJSWC since I took my infant daughter, Claire Page-Shiner, to a 1985 gathering at the Women's Centre marking the inclusion of the Equality Section [15] into the Canadian Charter of Rights and Freedoms. Claire's father, Rick Page, and I were in the midst of a challenge to NL law, under that section, to enable us to give our daughter the surname that joined our surnames in a declaration of equality. We were successful. To Claire and to our son, Ian, I have tried to demonstrate my commitment to equality in our home and through my paid and volunteer work toward social justice at Iris Kirby House, at Daybreak, with CUPE, with the NDP and with SJSWC. Now, my granddaughter, Margaret, is an extra inspiration for this goal.

My education about Deaf people's reality, in our community, began in the summer of 2013 when Jennifer Rimmer; her husband, Stephen; and her son, Jackson, came to Daybreak Parent Child Centre where I work as the Family Services Co-ordinator. Jennifer has shown me the challenges that she and Stephen face daily. As a result of witnessing Jennifer finding the courage it takes to navigate our hearing-centric society, I have chosen her as my inspiration. She believes in equality for women and for all members of the Deaf community. I am inspired by the breadth of her talents, the depth of her intelligence, and the strength of her commitment to work toward a diverse, respectful, inclusive society.

HERE IS JENNIFER RIMMER'S STORY:

My parents, Jo-Ann and Gary Sooley, were determined that my hearing brother and I would be given all the same opportunities but they did tell me that I would have to work harder than any hearing person. They warned me that others would judge me as being less capable because I am Deaf. Anyone who expressed pity that I was "Deaf and dumb" was quickly corrected. If I was offered a treat because I was "poor Jennifer," my mother would insist that I never be given anything that my brother was not also given. I received her clear message that I was equal to everyone else and everyone else was equal to me.

When I was kindergarten age, I had to leave my home community of Hearts Delight - Islington to become a resident at The Newfoundland School for the Deaf in St. John's. I have empathy for First Nations children whose only option for a formal education was to leave their homes. I remember crying, not wanting to stay in the dorm, but I also remember Cathy Lushman, an older student who was always active, always full of ideas of what we could do to make residence life more interesting.

PHOTO COURTESY OF JENNIFER RIMMER

I have suffered episodes of depression in my life. During one of those periods, as a young teenager, I saw Heather Whitestone, a Deaf woman, become Miss America. This changed my perspective on the possibilities for my life. Maybe I could integrate into the hearing world. I had begun to believe that Deaf people were inferior but I saw her being admired. At that time, I hadn't heard anything about Deaf people out in the world living fully included lives. I was too young to have the analysis to understand the harm of beauty pageants.

It was Ann Shortall, one of my high-school teachers, who introduced me to feminism and activism. In Women's Studies, at Memorial, I learned about the glass ceiling that stops so many women from reaching their potential and realized that the ceiling is much lower for me, a Deaf woman.

In 2010, I was the first Deaf person, who used American Sign Language exclusively to communicate, to graduate with a Bachelor of Arts degree from Memorial University, but I have not been able to obtain secure sustained employment where I can use my knowledge and skills.

Many Deaf leaders have left this province because services and opportunities, here, are so few. If I had given birth to a Deaf child, I would have moved out of this province. Absolutely. No doubt. I stayed so that my son, my husband, and I can have close contact with our extended families. I am committed to trying to change things, but it is a slow process. So far, I've managed to keep going. There have been times when it has become too emotional and I have become exhausted. I rest and I start again. I try to focus on what I can do.

Irving King Jordan, the first Deaf president of Gallaudet University, said that "Deaf people can do anything except hear," but our society places barriers in front of me. It is so hard to feel comfortable in a hearing world. I cannot access all the services that the hearing population takes for granted. It is a struggle to feel worthy.

I experience audism every day. I always have to remind people to do what is needed to make all services and events accessible for Deaf participants. There have been years of reminding!

I want to find funding to be a community-liaison worker to build trust between the Deaf and the Hearing, to get rid of the negative attitudes toward the Deaf, and to ensure that all services and opportunities are fully accessible to everyone. Our community would then be a better place for us all.

NOTES

PHOTO COURTESY OF ST. JOHN'S STATUS OF WOMEN COUNCIL ARCHIVES

JULY

2 SUNDAY

3 MONDAY

Canada Day Statutory Holiday

4 TUESDAY

5 WEDNESDAY

6 THURSDAY

7 FRIDAY

8 SATURDAY

On **July 1, 2015**, the St. John's Women's Centre began the annual tradition of laying a wreath during the Memorial Day ceremony to honour the women who served, and all of the families who loved and lost because of war.

9 SUNDAY ○

10 MONDAY

Orangemen's Day

11 TUESDAY

12 WEDNESDAY

13 THURSDAY

14 FRIDAY

15 SATURDAY

NOTES

16 SUNDAY 

17 MONDAY

18 TUESDAY

19 WEDNESDAY

20 THURSDAY

21 FRIDAY

22 SATURDAY

Transgender activist **KYRA REES**, in St. John's, took the provincial government to court to change the Vital Statistics Act to allow transgender people to change their birth certificate and government identification to match their gender identity and won on **July 22, 2015**.

23 SUNDAY 

24 MONDAY

25 TUESDAY

26 WEDNESDAY

27 THURSDAY

28 FRIDAY

29 SATURDAY

NOTES

JULY AUGUST

30 SUNDAY 

31 MONDAY

1 TUESDAY

2 WEDNESDAY

Regatta Day

AUGUST

3 THURSDAY

4 FRIDAY

5 SATURDAY

NOTES

LAURA WINTERS

PHOTO COURTESY OF LAURA WINTERS

Laura Winters is a community worker and activist, as well as a PhD candidate in Sociology at the University of New Brunswick.

She lives, works and researches in her home province of Newfoundland and Labrador, where she runs SHOP (Safe Harbour Outreach Project), a support service whose mandate is to advocate for the human rights of sex workers. SHOP operates from a harm reduction, human rights framework, based on the understanding that sex workers are the experts of their own lives and communities know what is best for themselves. Laura is constantly inspired by the strength, tenacity and resistance displayed by sex workers in NL and across Canada, in their fight for better laws, better working conditions, and a better society free from stigma and discrimination. Laura has immense respect for participants of SHOP, and she considers herself extremely lucky to have the privilege of working and researching with Newfoundlanders who do sex work. She would like to extend sincere thanks to everyone she has ever met who does sex work, for the collective education and perspective they have provided her; she knew nothing before listening to the voices of lived experience.

ON Nanny Francis

Francis is not my biological grandmother, but she's been Nan to me for nearly half my life. She has lived a life of great resistance; she was a single mother at a time when most women weren't, she worked outside the home at a time when most women didn't, and she still lives in her own home and cares for herself at an age when most women can't. And she does it all her way, with style.[1]

PHOTO COURTESY OF LAURA WINTERS

Me: "So, can you tell me about, I guess when your husband passed, and what happened?"

Francis: "Every time I would go in, Mom's neighbour used to say, put em [her four boys] in the orphanage, put em in the orphanage. And I couldn't put none of em in the orphanage. Not two, keep back two, no. The scandal [at Mount Cashel] was going on then, and I was some glad that I didn't put em in. I stood up for them.[2] The oldest was twelve, and youngest was only little over a year. People would say, Lots would take one or two children away from four. No way. If they had to take one of mine they'll take me first. I told em all to shut up! My neighbour…she used to always say, Put em in the orphanage, you can't manage four. I'd say No? I will then! See?"

1 *At ninety-two, Francis still refuses to leave the house without her hair set.*

2 *This is a point that Francis certainly doesn't mind bringing up to her adult children whenever she wants something done and they're not moving fast enough for her liking.*

Francis is a formidable, strong-headed woman; she's shown me a great deal of love and kindness…but I pity those who cross her. I asked her to give me an example of how she doesn't take shit from anyone: She recounted how, upon her return from church at St. Patrick's, her next door neighbour let her know that a gang of local boys was breaking into her yard, stealing her apples, and damaging her tree. This happened two Sundays in a row…

> Francis: "So I went out with the hatchet and I chopped it down! If they would leave it alone and let the apples grow a bit I could see a point… So I chopped it down! That's it! Then they came to the door, a little fella, looking for his cap [laughs] and I said, Get the hell outta here! You're not gettin no cap! I said, I never seen no cap. He said It's up in the tree! I said GO!!! So he went. I wouldn't give him his cap…I know I should…"
>
> Me: [laughs] "So there was a cap?"
>
> Francis: "Oh there was a cap alright! I took it and put it in the garbage [giggles]."

The apple-tree story is one of many examples of Francis fighting back; it was apples her way or no apples at all. There's something inherently feminist in that. From Francis, I've learned that what looks like weakness at first glance, can actually be power in disguise. Resistance from the underside is crafty and underhanded and camouflaged, it's resistance in tight spaces and hard circumstances. Like cutting down your own tree or not speaking up when your friend's husband hit you:

> Francis: "There would be my friends and my sister, and we all had a card game going every week. So he was married to my friend, and he'd always be drinking, and if he was drinking we only wanted the women playing. And we were in the other room playing and I got up. When I got into the kitchen, he hit me in the face! For God's sake, he said, Why

> can't I play! And I didn't say anything. Cuz if I did…you know, it would make a big scene. I said to myself I won't say nothing. I looked it over… because we all knew he was always hitting his wife, and it would've been embarrassing for her in front of everyone and she was my friend. She'd have nearly died from the embarrassment. And he would have loved that! So I wouldn't say nothing… I wouldn't give him the satisfaction [smiles]."

There was power in her calculated silence; it was resistance that at first glance looks nothing like resistance at all. It was the same with her mothering. For Francis, mothering her four boys was an act of great defiance—her husband had died, and raising four boys alone (let alone taking care of two elderly parents at the same time) was something everyone told her she couldn't, and shouldn't do. But she stood her ground, did it anyways…and she'd do it all again, too.

> Francis: "Oh I think if I had to go through it, I suppose I'd do it all again. I think I would. Yup. Cuz they [her sons] turned out good. I think if one of em had to turn out to be a drunkard, like his grandfather or his father, you know, I'd say, Well like he's like his father, but none of them were. I don't know why…if they pitied me or wha! [Laughs] Now…I think I'll have a drop of tea now while it's hot!"
>
> Me: "Proper thing."

AUGUST

6 SUNDAY

7 MONDAY ○

8 TUESDAY

9 WEDNESDAY

10 THURSDAY

11 FRIDAY

12 SATURDAY

STELLA BURRY: Born on **August 11, 1897**. Stella was a founding member of the Community Services Council in St. John's, and the Newfoundland and Labrador Association for the Aging.

AUGUST

13 SUNDAY

14 MONDAY 

15 TUESDAY

16 WEDNESDAY

17 THURSDAY

18 FRIDAY

19 SATURDAY

NOTES

AUGUST

20 SUNDAY

21 MONDAY 

22 TUESDAY

23 WEDNESDAY

AUGUST

24 THURSDAY

25 FRIDAY

26 SATURDAY

NOTES

AUGUST

27 SUNDAY

28 MONDAY

29 TUESDAY 

30 WEDNESDAY

AUGUST SEPTEMBER

31 THURSDAY

1 FRIDAY

2 SATURDAY

NOTES

MARY SHORTALL

Mary Shortall was elected as President of the Newfoundland & Labrador Federation of Labour (NLFL) in October, 2013. The NLFL represents 65,000 women and men, in more than twenty-five affiliated unions, who live and work in every community in NL.

Before being elected to NLFL, Mary was acting Regional Director for the Canadian Labour Congress (CLC). She had been the Newfoundland Representative for the CLC, since 2001.

She is a long-time member of Unifor, and was active in both the former unions CAW and CEP, and most recently served as Vice President of her Local at the CLC until her election.

Prior to working with the CLC, Mary was a Customer Sales and Service Agent with Air Canada (starting in 1977) and was involved with her union from 1982 until she went to the CLC. She served in many capacities with that union—Health and Safety Representative, Vice-Chair, Chair, and Regional Vice President on the Local Union Executive Board, national union educator, negotiator and human rights and women's committee member.

She has been a facilitator and curriculum developer throughout her union involvement and sees education and political action as the keys to activism. She is a passionate political and social activist, human rights advocate and, entwined throughout all that, Mary is a fiery feminist. She firmly believes that until all women are equal, then no one is free.

Mary makes time to enjoy the release that hiking, exercising, spending time with friends and family and taking to the road on her Harley Davidson brings to her life.

ON Nancy Riche

PHOTO BY THE TELEGRAM

On October 1, 2011, we lost a fierce fighter for women and workers. I lost my friend and mentor. Not a day goes by when I don't think about Nancy Riche. She continues to inspire me and push me to be as vigilant as I can in the struggle for a more equal, just, and fairer world.

As a young worker at Air Canada in the 80s, words like *feminism*, *equality*, *solidarity*, and *unions* were never in my vocabulary, nor at the time, my consciousness.

I can remember feeling, though, that it was not fair how some people were treated differently than others, especially women.

Nancy Riche was a frequent traveller during those days. I remember being a little in awe, and a little intimidated by her.

I learned about the union through those encounters, but never once did I envision being the elected president of an organization representing 65,000 unionized women and men. Nor did I realize then, that as a woman leader, there was an entire set of challenges that could make or break me and that I would learn that lesson, and other skills, by following Nancy's lead.

Nancy encouraged me to get involved. She failed to explain however that there was a "protocol" about how to do just that. That's because Nancy knew that sometimes protocol creates a barrier for women in the union, and if you want something, you just have to dive right in there and do it—"ask for forgiveness rather than permission"—my first invaluable lesson.

Now, many years later, I think how privileged I am to hold this position, and how important it is to be a voice for so many who have none, and to work as hard as I can for a more equal and fairer world. Not always an easy job, but always worth the struggle.

Nancy Riche's memory immediately conjures up many words: sister, friend and mentor, fearless, outrageous, impatient, feisty, irreverent, opinionated, gentle, caring, giving, loyal, demanding, gutsy, inclusive, blunt, and funny.

She was all that at any given time; her entire life was dedicated to equality, at any cost and against all odds.

She was a committed trade unionist and social justice advocate, whose feminism defined all her work. To her, women's issues were union issues. Union issues were social justice issues; and everything was political.

She became the secretary-treasurer of the Canadian Labour Congress, the president of the New Democratic Party, and the recipient of many awards for her work in labour rights, social justice and women's equality.

One thing that inspired me, more than anything else about Nancy, was her unwavering position that there was a direct link between the big and the small "P" political, and that no gains could be made in any arena without a good dose of both!

I heard her say, "There is joy in the struggle," and not only did she believe that, she instilled that joy in the struggle for so many of us. Even in retirement she would say, "After all these years of being a trade unionist, a feminist and a social democrat, I haven't changed my belief in what it is we are struggling for."

Nancy helped clear a path that saw many progressive changes that made a big difference to the economic and social realities for women and their families. Yet, the work is far from over.

The struggle continues to be real both inside and outside of the union, women's movement and the political arena. I have an obligation to continue her joyous struggle for equality.

Nancy has taught me to never shy away from being an advocate for women's issues above all else, because the victory comes when you build the political strength of women.

Through her, I have learned to pay attention to all sides of an issue, to be clear on my expectations, to be prepared, to not compromise nor back down, to bring other women along, to keep a sense of humour, and above all hope.

Today—when women are denied equal rights all over this globe, and the struggle seems futile—I step back and reflect on all the extraordinary women who have been instrumental in transforming our world.

My wish—to be remembered the same way Nancy wanted, when she once replied, "I hopefully opened the doors for other women to move into leadership positions, because it's stupid not to, quite frankly. Are you going to be president and then leave with no other women there? It makes no sense. If I have inspired any women to get active in the women's movement or the labour movement, I think that's great."

If I have inspired women not only to see the joy in the struggle, but to join it—then I will have achieved what my dear sister would have called, "taking our rightful place at the front of the room!"

SEPTEMBER

3 SUNDAY

4 MONDAY

Labour Day

5 TUESDAY

6 WEDNESDAY ◯

SEPTEMBER

7 THURSDAY

8 FRIDAY

9 SATURDAY

NOTES

SEPTEMBER

10 SUNDAY

11 MONDAY

12 TUESDAY

13 WEDNESDAY

SEPTEMBER

14 THURSDAY

15 FRIDAY

16 SATURDAY

NOTES

SEPTEMBER

17 SUNDAY

18 MONDAY

19 TUESDAY

20 WEDNESDAY 

SEPTEMBER

21 THURSDAY

22 FRIDAY

Muharram/Islamic New Year | Equinox

23 SATURDAY

The Newfoundland Status of Women's Council held its first general meeting on **September 18, 1972**.

SEPTEMBER

24 SUNDAY

25 MONDAY

26 TUESDAY

27 WEDNESDAY 

SEPTEMBER

28 THURSDAY

29 FRIDAY

30 SATURDAY

JULIA SALTER EARLE: Born in St. John's on **September 20, 1878**, and was known for her advocacy work to improve conditions for the working classes. During the Depression, she led a march of about 500 unemployed men through St. John's to the Colonial Building. She became President of the Ladies Brand of the Newfoundland Industrial Workers Association.

LISA MOORE

PHOTO BY NATHALIE MARSH

Lisa Moore is the author of the novels ***Alligator***, ***Caught***, and ***February***, the short-story collections ***Degrees of Nakedness*** and ***Open***, and the stage adaptation of her novel ***February***. Moore's first young-adult novel, ***Flannery***, was published in April 2016. She is a professor of Creative Writing at Memorial University.

There's a line, thin as a laser light, between beauty and fear. I first saw Anahareo Döelle climbing two billowing curtains of silk in the Arts and Culture Centre at the annual *Divas Do Christmas* concert. I crunched in my seat and ran my hands over my legs, palms sweating. My heart was beating as fast as a sparrow's. I tried not to look. I slapped one hand over my eyes, but then peeked through my fingers.

I couldn't *not* look.

And so I watched as this feather-light, licorice-whip-flexible aerial artist climbed toward the thousands of pin-prick yellow lights in the ceiling above the stage. The ceiling, so far away.

Anahareo wove a silk ladder for herself, from the twisting, swinging curtains of fabric. Footholds slipped away as soon as she stepped from them. She swung her legs over her head, and her hands over her legs. She gripped the silks and her body was like liquid, streaming upward. Whipping around, sliding, braiding the ropes with her body. She held tight, or she hardly seemed to hold on at all.

ON Anahareo Döelle

PHOTO COURTESY OF MARIAN FRANCES WHITE

The silks rippled over her like a waterfall, or they cradled her. She was a starfish floating in the dark above us. The silks were a kind of second skin, through which we saw a knee emerge, her hand, her beautiful, smiling face. The silks demand a discipline and incredible physical strength in order to allow for a pure freedom of self-expression.

Who is this young woman, fearlessly defying gravity? Climbing higher and higher?

Anahareo Döelle grew up in St. John's and had gone to kindergarten with her hair in two neat braids, a big smile, a little knapsack, and a pin on her jacket lapel, affixed by her mother, the feminist activist, poet, and filmmaker, Marian White. The pin on Anahareo's jacket (though she could not yet read it!) proclaimed the advice: Question Authority!

Anahareo's father, Beni Malone, is a respected performance artist, a clown. He is the inventor of Newfoundland's own Wonderbolt Circus. Beni had taken Anahareo on tour with the circus at the age of twelve. Anahareo worked both backstage, preparing props, and she made stage appearances as the assistant robot called Bucky. She did flips and cartwheels while her father zipped around on a unicycle, or strutted on stilts, or juggled flames and ate them.

But her debut stage performances in the circus happened when Anahareo was three. She opened the show by introducing her father, except she called it "im-pro-ducing."

At the age of fifteen, Anahareo found herself watching a documentary on television about Circe-de-Soleil, perhaps the most famous circus in the world. When the documentary was over, she got a pen and a piece of paper. She wrote to Circe-de-Soleil and told them she wanted to join.

"I knew then," she says, "this is what I wanted to do."

When I arrive at Anahareo's house to talk about her life in the circus, I find her two young daughters picking up a stack of cards they had, obviously just seconds before, tossed into the air. Anahareo's seven-month-old son is watching, gleeful, on the sidelines. She scoops him up, on the way to the patio, where she rocks him to sleep in her arms as we chat in the delicious sun.

Anahareo tells me that after two years of study at Memorial University and time spent with Canada World Youth in Jamaica, she gained acceptance at the prestigious National Circus School of Montreal.

"It was three years of study, eight hours a day," she tells me. "It was very demanding physically and emotionally." But it is clear she loved her experience there. Aerials became her main focus of study at the school.

"Anything off the ground," she says, "I majored in hoops and minored in silks." She tells me that the silks are like long curtains she can climb. The hoops hang in the air suspended by a single rope. The hoop is on a swivel so it spins and is three-dimensional. Sometimes it looks like the moon and it allows for work with a partner. Anahareo tells me she likes to create a story with her work. She says the silks can look spectacular, soft and flowy. She is able to wrap herself up in them at the top and drop all the way to the bottom.

After the National Circus School of Montreal, Anahareo performed all over Europe, spending a lot of time on the cabaret circuit in Germany, with forays into Japan.

Eventually, she and her husband, Marco Döelle (who works in film), decided to return to Newfoundland to raise their children, and Anahareo opened her own school called "I Fly Aerial Arts." She sometimes brings her children to work with her when she teaches. She brings in international artists to conduct workshops with her students and she herself is performing frequently. She has also trained as a yoga and palates instructor.

"Right now I teach ages five to sixty-seven. I have forty students, fifteen classes a week," Anahareo says.

I think about the moment of the performance I had seen when

Anahareo had seemed to reach the ceiling, so far above our heads. And I also thought about the moment when her young daughters must have thrown those playing cards in the air, just before I arrived to do the interview.

The sheer freeing joy of tossing all those cards.

I thought of the second when those cards would have been suspended, just before their fluttering descent.

Anahareo's agility, strength, and grace, climbing those silks seemed like a lesson or metaphor or a gift the audience could take away. Once she had reached the top, she let go and tumbled down from that great height, unravelling from the silk curtains that had suspended her, flipping and twisting and spinning. The entire audience drew a single gasp.

This act of letting go seemed to be saying: Live life like this!

I simultaneously loved what I was seeing and I wished it would be over. I wanted her to be safe. I was thrilled and afraid and also, well, just thrilled. I thought about her mother. I thought about my own children. I thought about what it means to make art with your body as the tool, mind and body together.

I thought about the verb "amaze." How often do people provoke amazement in us? How amazement opens us up. How it stops us short and demands we feel the sensation of being alive. It demands we toss all our cards in the air and question authority and not be afraid and that we open our eyes.

OCTOBER

1 SUNDAY

2 MONDAY

3 TUESDAY

4 WEDNESDAY

OCTOBER

5 THURSDAY ◯

6 FRIDAY

7 SATURDAY

NOTES

OCTOBER

8 SUNDAY

9 MONDAY

Thanksgiving Day

10 TUESDAY

11 WEDNESDAY

OCTOBER

12 THURSDAY

13 FRIDAY

14 SATURDAY

NOTES

OCTOBER

15 SUNDAY

16 MONDAY

17 TUESDAY

18 WEDNESDAY

19 THURSDAY 

20 FRIDAY

21 SATURDAY

MARGARET IRIS DULEY: Newfoundland's first novelist. Her feminist writing explored topics of divorce, female independence, and sexuality. Her first work, *The Eyes of the Gull*, was published on **October 18, 1936**.

OCTOBER

22 SUNDAY

23 MONDAY

24 TUESDAY

25 WEDNESDAY

OCTOBER

26 THURSDAY

27 FRIDAY

28 SATURDAY

NOTES

OCTOBER

29 SUNDAY

30 MONDAY

31 TUESDAY

Halloween

1 WEDNESDAY

NOVEMBER

2 THURSDAY

3 FRIDAY

4 SATURDAY ○

Newfoundland and Labrador women cast votes for the first time in a general election on **October 29, 1928**.

ZITA COBB

PHOTO BY LUTHER CAVERLY

Zita Cobb is CEO of the Shorefast Foundation, a registered Canadian charity, and founder and Innkeeper of the Fogo Island Inn. Growing up on Fogo Island, a remote fishing community off the northeast coast of Newfoundland, Zita developed a deep belief in the inherent value of place and a profound respect for the human ways of knowing that emerge from respectful relationships with nature, culture, and community. At age sixteen, she left to study business and became a senior finance professional in the high-technology industry. Most notably, Zita worked at JDS Fitel (subsequently JDS Uniphase) in Ottawa from 1981 to 2001, where she helped build one of the most successful high-tech innovators in history.

Cobb retired from her business career in 2001 and returned to Fogo Island where the cod fishery had collapsed and the population had fallen from the 5,500 of her youth to 2,500. Feeling compelled to act, she founded the Shorefast Foundation (www.shorefast.org) with her brothers Anthony and Alan Cobb. Shorefast Foundation is a registered charity of Canada, and operates as a social enterprise that employs business-minded means to achieve social ends. Recognizing that traditional charity in the form of monetary handouts would not contribute to long-term cultural, social, and economic resiliency for Fogo Island, the Foundation's goal was to leverage an initial investment to create culturally-rich, community-owned economic assets. Shorefast's most significant projects to date are the award-winning Fogo Island Inn (www.fogoislandinn.ca), Fogo Island Arts (www.fogoislandarts.ca), and, most recently, The Fogo Island Shop (www.fogoislandshop.ca). These diverse projects draw on the traditional talents of Fogo Islanders to help generate the social, cultural, and economic capital necessary for Fogo Island to thrive in the twenty-first century and beyond.

Above all, Zita believes that the key to resilience for rural communities lies in the specificity of place: rediscovering intellectual heritage and cultural wisdom, and fostering the talent, knowledge, and abundance of possibility that already exist naturally in our communities. She remains guided by her belief that nature and culture are the two great garments of human life, and that business and technology are the two great tools that can and should serve them.

ON Fogo Island Women

"Islands represent both paradise and purgatory."
—J. EDWARD CHAMBERLAIN

For Fogo Islanders, our remotenes —our "islandness"—is inextricably ingrained in our sense of being. We have a way of knowing and a way of existing that is born specifically of our island home and the realities of making a living off of the tumultuous North Atlantic. A life lived at the edge of the North American continent was a life lived at the edge of life itself. The next wave might knock you overboard. The next catch might not be enough to feed your family. Your mother might not survive the next childbirth. Your next sibling might not see their first birthday. Existing in this place, you knew that the next closest shore and the next closest help was rarely, if ever, on the way. Laying in bed at night, you felt grateful that those you loved were safe in the harbour. Tomorrow would be tomorrow.

Despite the challenges of remoteness, Fogo Island has thrived as a fishing community for centuries. Our ancestors came here for the cod and stayed for the cod, fishing these icy waters for generations. Our isolation from the mainland made us fiercely independent with a way of knowing that emerged from centuries of intimate encounters with place. For the most part, our remoteness was a beautiful thing: it made us…us.

But remoteness became a stinging, painful thing in times of medical need. Fishing hooks, rogue ropes, boats tossed at sea, and an unwatched toddler falling into the clutches of the ocean were all recipes for loss of limb and life. Children were trying to be born in a place without doctors and hospitals. Houses were catching on fire, skin became burned, wounds became infected; teeth, kidneys, nerves and hearts gave out. Medical need arose brutally and unexpectedly and ran the gamut of all that could possibly be "wrong" with a human being. And when need arose, whatever it was, nurses and midwives carried the burden of response and care.

Like many remote places, the nurses and midwives of Fogo Island were women (some formally trained, most not). They stood in the place of doctors as the medical providers in our community. When moments of medical need arose, whether expected in the case of a childbirth or unexpected in the case of an accident, someone ran to get one of these women. In my home community of Joe Batt's Arm, these were women like Mrs. Rose Penton and Mrs. Jessie Coffin (both midwives), and Mrs. Margaret Cobb, a trained nurse. Every community on the island had their own Mrs. Rose, Mrs. Jessie, and Mrs. Margaret. I have often wondered if women like these understood just how much rested on their shoulders. Did they lay in dread each night of the next knock on the door?

They had a quiet confidence, care, and focus that was calming. You felt better after they looked at you. They never said things like, "everything is going to be fine." They knew and we knew that everything might not be fine. My best friend, Margaret Emberley, was one of ten children; she was one of the four that lived beyond the age of two. Despite the best efforts of women like Mrs. Rose and Mrs. Jessie, they found themselves playing coroner to six little bodies in just that one house. And the day that young Anthony Penton's five-year-old body was pulled from the harbour drowned, one of those women would have been called. They did what they could for the dead and dying and they did what they could for the living left to grieve. Despite being a community divided by religious differences, the care offered by these women crossed all boundaries—religious and otherwise.

Sometimes, their medical interventions ended well. Children and mothers survived childbirth. Wounds closed. Burns healed. Bones mended. But through it all, we accepted that what was going to happen was part of a larger scheme. And we had the conviction that what *could* be done *had* been done through these steadfast women.

We never threw parties or offered gifts to thank those who lent such unselfish and constant service. Our gratitude, appreciation, and reverence for them was exceptionally palpable but rarely ever spoken. We regarded them as superior mortals, and our respect for them would have seemed cheapened by overt displays of appreciation. That we treasured them and depended on them was deeply felt and known.

Today, Fogo Island has a medical centre, an ambulance, and a volunteer fire department which help to mitigate the impact of medical emergencies. But these first responders are still members of this small community; members of a community where families have known each other for centuries. They carry on where women like Mrs. Rose, Mrs. Jessie, and Mrs. Margaret have left off. Like them, first responders leap to help, knowing full well that the people they come upon will be people they know deeply. Like their urban counterparts, these responders suffer the trauma of seeing things people shouldn't have to see, but they also suffer the additional anxiety and trauma of attending to someone they are deeply connected with through culture and time. Our communities couldn't function without these first volunteers and professionals. We owe them everything. They are always on watch.

And we still take comfort from the women who are already gone, like Mrs. Rose, Mrs. Jessie, and Mrs. Margaret. We feel their attentive and loving gaze, and the bright light of their steadfastness still gives us courage.

NOVEMBER

5 SUNDAY

Guy Fawkes Night (Bonfire Night) | Daylight Saving Time Ends

6 MONDAY

7 TUESDAY

8 WEDNESDAY

NOVEMBER

9 THURSDAY

10 FRIDAY

11 SATURDAY

Remembrance Day

NOTES

NOVEMBER

12 SUNDAY

13 MONDAY

Remembrance Day Holiday

14 TUESDAY

15 WEDNESDAY

NOVEMBER

16 THURSDAY

17 FRIDAY

18 SATURDAY 

NOTES

NOVEMBER

19 SUNDAY

20 MONDAY

21 TUESDAY

22 WEDNESDAY

NOVEMBER

23 THURSDAY

24 FRIDAY

25 SATURDAY

NOTES

NOVEMBER

26 SUNDAY 

27 MONDAY

28 TUESDAY

29 WEDNESDAY

NOVEMBER DECEMBER

30 THURSDAY

1 FRIDAY

2 SATURDAY

NOTES

KAETLYN OSMOND

PHOTO BY SKATE CANADA

Following her sister, Natasha, at the age of two, Kaetlyn joined the Ice Crystals Figure Skating Club in Marystown, Newfoundland. There, she began a career that brought her across the country and around the world. She made the move to Montreal at the age of eight to train with Josée Picard who brought her to her very first Junior Nationals and brought her to her first big win in the sport at only ten years old. Not long after, the sisters made their final move for the sport and to be with their parents in Edmonton, Alberta, training with Ravi Walia, at the Ice Palace Figure Skating Club. Since making the move to Edmonton, she has won seven national medals, three of which were gold. In 2013, she made her big debut on the senior international stage. Kaetlyn won the Nebelhorn Trophy and Skate Canada International. She also won her first Senior National title, earning her a spot at her first World Championships where she placed eighth overall. In 2014, she became the two-time National champion, earning her a spot on the 2014 Olympic Team, which earned her a silver medal in the Figure Skating team event. After overcoming injuries since the Olympic games, she continues to train and compete, earning another Nebelhorn Trophy win and a bronze at the 2016 National Championships.

ON Natasha Osmond

A Newfoundland woman that has been my biggest inspiration is someone that not many people will know, but someone I know and look up to every single day. She may not have made any big, well-known miracles happen, or changed the lives of millions, but she didn't need to: she changed my life and she made miracles happen for me.

This woman is my inspiration, my role model, my best friend, and she is my sister, Natasha Osmond. I got the chance not many people can say in their lives—I had the opportunity to grow up alongside my biggest inspiration, sharing my entire life with her. Natasha is three years older than me, making her five years old when she changed my life forever.

Long before I can remember, I watched my sister push herself on the ice, learning to be a figure skater. I wanted to be just like her. I found my role model when I was two years old, and I was always striving to be as good as her. She could do anything that anyone asked of her, and if she couldn't, she found a way to make it work.

She sacrificed by leaving her friends—and for a little while, her family—to make her dreams come true. I watched her push every day to reach perfection. I watched her fight through her fears and compete in front of a crowd. She competed in singles, and with a partner in both pairs and singles, making it to the National level in all three disciplines, which is something that is rare in figure skating.

I lucked out one year and got the opportunity to compete against my sister. Can you imagine how amazing and nerve-wracking that would be? Competing against someone you have looked up to, always trying to be as good as, since long before you can remember? I had the chance to compete against Natasha twice before she hung up her skates for good. Both times I lucked out and placed just ahead of her, something I really couldn't believe. At only thirteen years old, I managed to do something I always dreamed of—being as good as my sister.

When I competed against her those two times, I learned so much more about my sister than I ever knew before. I thought I had always looked up to her because of her ability to skate so beautifully on the ice. After she hung up her skates, I realized what really made her such an inspiration to me. Natasha always held herself so strong and professional. She never let anything get to her; even having her little sister beat her didn't drop her spirits. My role model then became my biggest supporter; how did I become so lucky?

Even with Natasha no longer on the ice, it never changed how I look up to her. She changed her views from the ice to a career and a family. Natasha now has a son of her own, a family, a home, and going to school to kick-start a career. At only twenty-three years old, my sister shows me everyday that with a lot of hard work, anything I ever want is within my reach. I see how hard she studies to keep her grades up in school, at the same time she is teaching a young boy how to walk, run, talk, and skate on his own.

Nothing was ever easy for her, in skating or in school. I see how much she focuses and puts hard work in the place of natural talent. Natasha is the hardest working, most loving mom, daughter, and sister that my family has ever had.

She inspires and encourages me every day, changing my life with each second. She understands the struggles that I go through in my life with injuries, exhaustion, and doubt. She knows how to get me out of my head and back on my feet even at the worst of times. I look up to her, and she pushes me. She advises me on all parts of my life—friends, family, school, and skating. She is always there for me to talk to when I need to. I don't know how I became so lucky to grow up with such an amazing sister that doubles as an incredible role model. Natasha made all my dreams come true just because she was always there for me.

NOTES

PHOTO COURTESY OF ST. JOHN'S STATUS OF WOMEN COUNCIL ARCHIVES

DECEMBER

3 SUNDAY ◯

4 MONDAY

5 TUESDAY

6 WEDNESDAY

DECEMBER

7 THURSDAY

8 FRIDAY

9 SATURDAY

KATHY DUNDERDALE becomes the first female premier in Newfoundland and Labrador history on **December 3, 2010**.

DECEMBER

10 SUNDAY

11 MONDAY

12 TUESDAY

13 WEDNESDAY

First Day of Hanukkah

DECEMBER

14 THURSDAY

15 FRIDAY

16 SATURDAY

NOTES

DECEMBER

17 SUNDAY

18 MONDAY 

19 TUESDAY

20 WEDNESDAY

Last Day of Hanukkah

DECEMBER

21 THURSDAY

Winter Solstice

22 FRIDAY

23 SATURDAY

Tibb's Eve (Tipp's Eve)

NOTES

DECEMBER

24 SUNDAY

Christmas Eve

25 MONDAY

Christmas Day

26 TUESDAY 

Boxing Day | St. Stephen's Day (The traditional beginning of mummering in Newfoundland)

27 WEDNESDAY

DECEMBER

28 THURSDAY

29 FRIDAY

30 SATURDAY

31 SUNDAY

New Year's Eve

NOTES

PHOTO COURTESY OF ST. JOHN'S STATUS OF WOMEN ARCHIVES